COOTER

REST IN PEACE
1996-2008

A B C D E
F G H I J
K L M N O
P Q R S T
U V X Y Z

ABCDE
FGHIJ
KLMNO
PQRST
UVXYZ

BEN EINE
ALPHABET PIECES

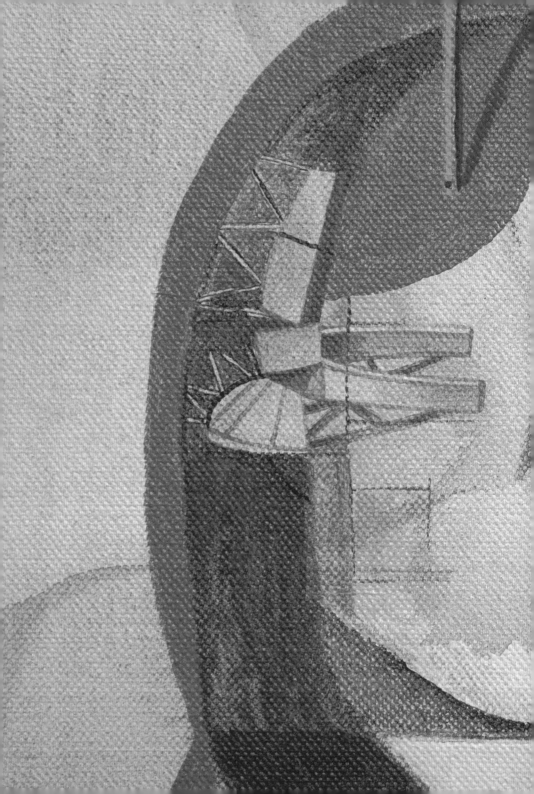

DOZE GREEN WORKING IN UP LIVE/WORK STUDIO

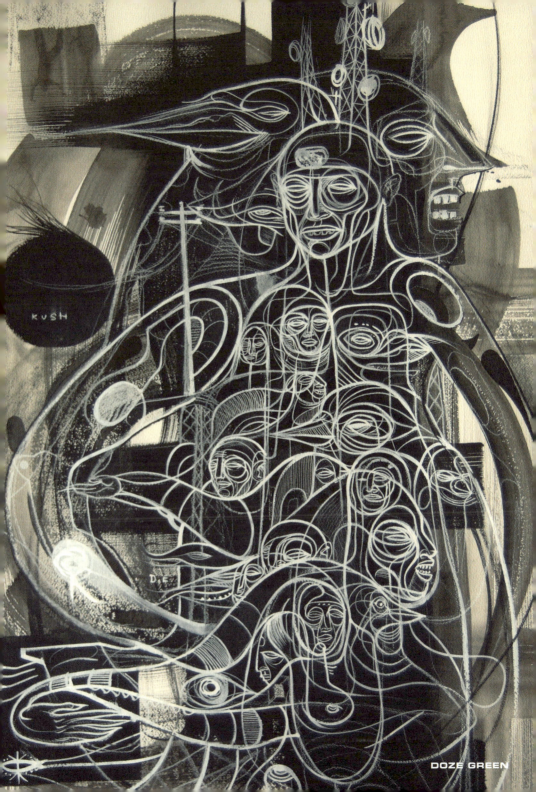

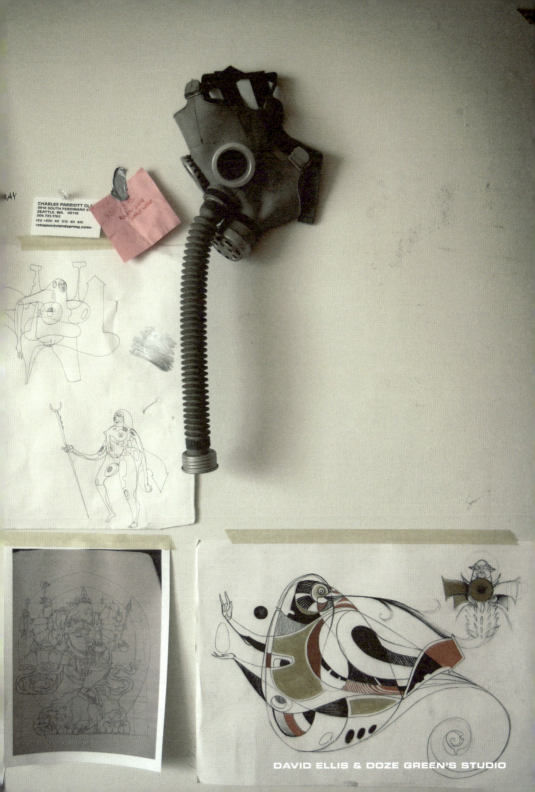

DAVID ELLIS

CRAOLA WALRUS TOY

SAM FLORES
FATIMA

JEREMY FISH
BARRY THE BEAVER

ANDY JENKINS
LETTUS BEE

GET SMALL SERIES

DAVID CHOE
BOOKSHELF

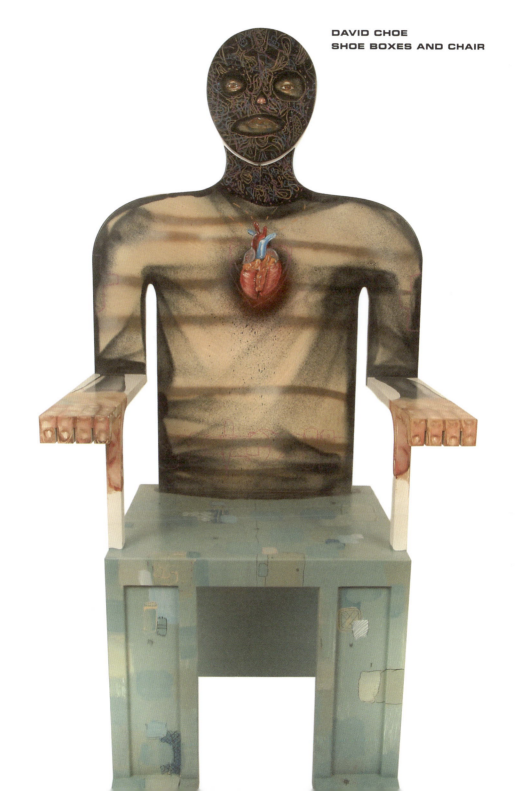

DAVID CHOE
SHOE BOXES AND CHAIR

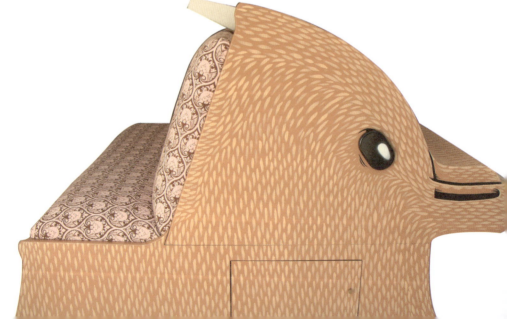

JEREMY FISH
TURTLE TABLE AND BUNNY SOFA

SAM FLORES
BAR STOOL AND BAR

SAM FLORES BAR

**HERBERT BAGLIONE
DRESSER**

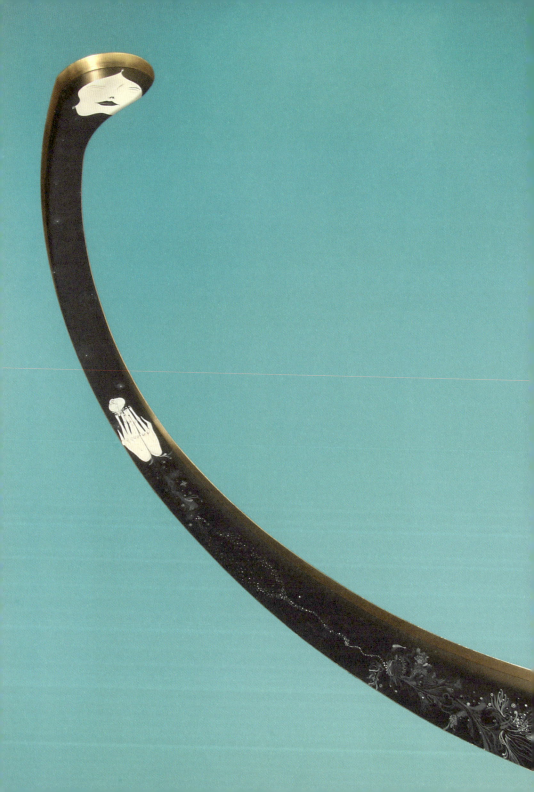

HERBERT BAGLIONE
DINING TABLE

TIFFANY BOZIC
BEDROOM SET

TIFFANY BOZIC
VANITY

**SABER
DRESSER**

MIKE GIANT
HALLWAY CHAIR
AND PEDESTAL TABLES

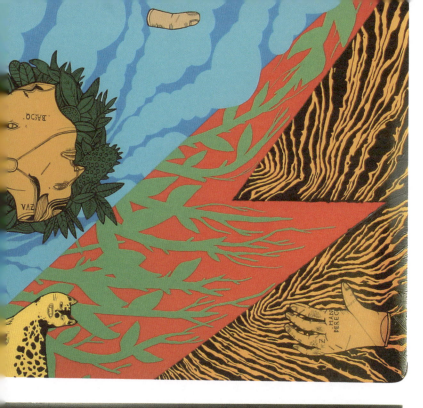

**BASCO
BUFFET TABLE**

RETNA PAINTING

DATE FARMERS AD FOR UP

CRAOLA AD FOR UP

USUGROW AD FOR UP

SABER IN LONDON

DAVID CHOE X SABER MURAL IN LONDON

MIKE MAXWELL SHOW AT FIFTY24PDX

BASCO SHOW AT FIFTY24PDX

SLICK
SHOW SET UP AT FIFTY24SF

ARMSROCK SETTING UP AT FIFTY24SF

D*FACE STREET INSTALLATION

JEREMY FISH IN ROME

UPPER PLAYGROUND X adidas originals

CAR CRASH AT FIFTY24SF GALLERY

UPPER PLAYGROUND VOL. II

COOTER R.I.P.
PHOTO: LISA REVELLI

UP STORES
BERKELEY: JUDO
LONDON: CHRISTIAN STEWART
PORTLAND: STEPHEN POZGAY

BASCO SHOW AT FIFTY24PDX
PHOTO: KAI AITCHSON

SABER IN LONDON
PHOTO: KIMBERLY VERDE

SAM FLORES & JEREMY FISH IN TAIWAN
PHOTO: MATT REVELLI

SABER X DAVID CHOE MURAL IN LONDON
PHOTO: KIMBERLY VERDE

MIKE MAXWELL SHOW AT FIFTY24PDX
PHOTO: KAI AITCHSON

JEREMY FISH IN ROME
PHOTO: RICK MARR

CAR CRASH AT FIFTY24SF
PHOTO: CARLOS MENDEZ

FRANCISCO ROBLES THANKS:
KIMBERLY VERDE AND THE FIFTY24SF GALLERY CREW
JOSEPH HASTINGS
MIKE MEHAFEY
JOHN SHEPARD
ALAN WAUGH
DAVID CRAIG

DESIGN BY JARROD BRYAN
ALL PHOTOGRAPHY BY JON DRAGONETTE EXCEPT WHERE NOTED

ALL RIGHTS RESERVED. NO PART OF THIS BOOK MAY BE REPRODUCED OR TRANSMITTED IN ANY FORM OR ANY MEANS, ELECTRONIC
MECHANICAL, INCLUDING PHOTOCOPY, RECORDING OR ANY OTHER INFORMATION
STORAGE AND RETRIEVAL SYSTEM, WITHOUT THE WRITTEN PERMISSION FROM THE PUBLISHER AND THE ARTIST.
PRINTED IN HONG KONG

MAIN OFFICE:
1661 TENNESSEE ST. UNIT 3F
SAN FRANCISCO, CA 94107
PH: 415.252.0144 FX: 415.252.1482
WWW.UPPERPLAYGROUND.COM
WWW.FIFTY24SF.COM